Novena

to

St. Anne

A 9-Day Devotion for Faith and Miracles

Novena to St. Anne

Copyright © 2023 By Dave Watson

ISBN: 9798853316614

Cover illustration and content by Dave Watson

For permissions or inquiries, please contact djb20182018@gmail.com

Table of Contents

Introduction

Welcome to "Novena to St. Anne," a book dedicated to exploring the profound spiritual journey of praying the Novena to St. Anne. Within these pages, we delve into the rich history, significance, and transformative power of this devotional practice. Whether you are already familiar with St. Anne or just discovering her inspiring presence, this book aims to guide you through a nine-day prayer journey that can deepen your faith and foster a closer relationship with this beloved saint.

St. Anne holds a special place in Christian tradition as the mother of the Blessed Virgin Mary and the grandmother of Jesus Christ. Despite limited mentions in the Bible, her influence as a saintly figure has captured the hearts of countless individuals throughout history. As we embark on this novena, we will explore the life and background of St. Anne, her role in Christian tradition, and the patronages and devotions associated with her.

In the first chapter, we uncover the power of novenas. Novenas have been a cherished practice within the Catholic Church and other Christian traditions, offering a focused and intentional way to seek divine intercession and guidance. We discuss the history and significance of novenas and delve into the benefits they bring to our spiritual lives.

Chapter 2 is dedicated to introducing St. Anne as a saintly figure. We learn about her life and background, gaining insight into her character and virtues. St. Anne's steadfast faith, unwavering patience, enduring hope, boundless love, profound humility, and inner strength serve as guiding lights for our own spiritual journey.

Chapter 3 is the heart of the book, providing a comprehensive guide to praying the Novena to St. Anne. We delve into the preparation, setting intentions, and the nine-day prayer structure of the novena. Alongside this, we explore the various practices and customs associated with the novena, encouraging a more immersive and meaningful experience.

The subsequent section delve into each of the nine days of the novena. Each day focuses on a specific virtue or aspect of St. Anne's life, offering reflections to deepen our understanding and prayers to express our desires and intentions. These reflections and prayers aim to inspire and uplift, drawing us closer to St. Anne's example and the divine grace she embodies.

Finally, in the concluding section, we express our gratitude and encouragement, inviting readers to continue their devotion to St. Anne beyond the novena. Additionally, we provide an appendix with additional prayers and resources, a glossary to define key terms, an index for easy reference, acknowledgments, and an author's note with personal reflections or messages.

As you embark on this journey of prayer and devotion to St. Anne, may this book be a source of inspiration, guidance, and comfort. May it deepen your faith, strengthen your connection to St. Anne, and ultimately bring you closer to the divine. Open your heart, embrace the transformative power of the novena, and let St. Anne's intercession guide you on the path to spiritual growth and grace.

Together, let us embark on this nine-day journey of prayer and discover the immense blessings that await us through the "Novena to St. Anne."

About St. Anne

St. Anne, often referred to as "Anne, the mother of Mary," holds a significant place in Christian tradition, particularly within Catholicism. While there is limited information about her in the Bible, her role as the mother of the Virgin Mary and the grandmother of Jesus Christ has made her an influential figure in religious devotion and piety.

The name "Anne" is of Hebrew origin and means "grace" or "favor." According to apocryphal writings, Anne was born in Bethlehem and belonged to the tribe of Levi. She is believed to have married Joachim, a devout and righteous man from Nazareth. Together, they lived a life of deep faith and devotion to God.

One of the most well-known aspects of St. Anne's life is her miraculous conception of Mary. The couple, Joachim and Anne, faced the heartache of being childless for many years. However, through divine intervention, Anne conceived a child in her old age. This miraculous conception was seen as a sign of God's favor and grace.

St. Anne's daughter, Mary, went on to become the mother of Jesus. As such, St. Anne holds a significant place in the lineage of Christ and the unfolding of salvation history. Her role as the grandmother of Jesus has led to her being venerated as a powerful intercessor and a source of maternal love and protection.

While St. Anne's life is not extensively documented in the Bible, her importance within Christian tradition and devotion has led to various legends and stories about her. These stories often emphasize her virtues, including her unwavering faith, patience, humility, love, and strength. St. Anne is regarded as a model of virtuous living and an inspiration for believers seeking to deepen their relationship with God.

Throughout history, St. Anne has been recognized as the patroness of several groups and causes. She is revered as the patron saint of mothers, women in labor, grandparents, homemakers, cabinetmakers, and miners, among others. Many churches and shrines around the world are dedicated to her, drawing pilgrims and devotees who seek her intercession and guidance.

The devotion to St. Anne includes various prayers, novenas, and devotional practices aimed at seeking her intercession and cultivating a closer relationship with her. The Novena to St. Anne, in particular, is a cherished tradition where believers pray for nine consecutive days, reflecting on St. Anne's virtues and seeking her intercession for their intentions.

St. Anne's influence extends beyond specific religious affiliations, as her loving and maternal nature resonates with people from various backgrounds. She is seen as a compassionate and understanding figure, ready to embrace and guide those who turn to her for assistance.

In summary, St. Anne, the mother of Mary and the grandmother of Jesus, is a revered figure in Christian tradition. Her virtuous life, her role in the birth of Mary, and her connection to Jesus have made her a beloved saint and a powerful intercessor. Devotion to St. Anne offers solace, inspiration, and a profound example of faith, love, and grace.

Purpose of the Novena

The Novena to St. Anne serves multiple purposes, all aimed at fostering a deeper spiritual connection with St. Anne and seeking her intercession. The primary purposes of the novena include:

1. Seeking St. Anne's Intercession: The novena provides a structured and intentional way to seek St. Anne's intercession for specific intentions. Believers turn to St. Anne, recognizing her as a powerful intercessor before God, and ask for her prayers and assistance in their needs and challenges. The novena allows individuals to present their petitions and desires to St. Anne with faith and confidence, trusting in her maternal love and her ability to intercede on their behalf.

2. Deepening Faith and Devotion: Praying the novena to St. Anne offers an opportunity to deepen one's faith and cultivate a stronger devotion to this beloved saint. By reflecting on St. Anne's virtues, studying her life and example, and immersing oneself in the prayers and practices of the novena, individuals can grow in their understanding and appreciation of St. Anne's role in salvation history and her significance as a model of faith. The novena encourages believers to develop a personal relationship with St. Anne, fostering a sense of closeness and reliance on her spiritual guidance.

3. Embodying St. Anne's Virtues: Each day of the novena typically focuses on a specific virtue or aspect of St. Anne's life. By contemplating and meditating on these virtues, individuals are inspired to embody them in their own lives. St. Anne's faith, patience, hope, love, humility, and strength serve as powerful examples for believers to emulate. The novena offers a framework for personal reflection and growth, inviting individuals to align their thoughts, actions, and attitudes with the virtues exemplified by St. Anne.

4. Finding Comfort and Support: The Novena to St. Anne provides a source of solace and support for those facing challenges, difficulties, or uncertainties. St. Anne is seen as a compassionate and understanding figure, a loving grandmother who extends her care and protection to those who seek her intercession. By turning to St. Anne in prayer, individuals often find comfort in knowing that they are not alone in their struggles. The novena becomes a source of encouragement and reassurance, reminding believers of St. Anne's maternal presence and her willingness to help and guide them through life's trials.

5. Expressing Gratitude: The novena also serves as a means to express gratitude to St. Anne for her intercession and blessings received. Throughout the nine days of the novena, individuals have an opportunity to offer thanks for answered prayers, blessings received, and the spiritual growth experienced through their devotion to St. Anne. Gratitude becomes

an integral part of the novena, fostering a sense of appreciation and a deeper recognition of the grace and goodness bestowed through St. Anne's intercession.

In essence, the Novena to St. Anne combines prayer, reflection, and devotion to seek St. Anne's intercession, deepen faith, embody virtues, find solace, and express gratitude. It is a powerful spiritual practice that allows individuals to connect with St. Anne and experience the transformative power of her intercession in their lives.

Chapter One

The Power of Novenas

1.1 Understanding Novenas

Novenas are a cherished and time-honored tradition within the Catholic Church and other Christian denominations. Derived from the Latin word "novem," meaning "nine," a novena is a period of focused and deliberate prayer consisting of nine consecutive days. The practice of praying a novena is rooted in biblical and historical traditions, and it holds a special place in the hearts of believers seeking a deeper connection with God and the saints.

The concept of novenas finds its origins in the Acts of the Apostles in the Bible. After Jesus' ascension into heaven, the apostles, along with Mary gathered in the upper room and dedicated themselves to prayer for nine days before the outpouring of the Holy Spirit on Pentecost. This period of intense prayer and waiting set the precedent for the practice of novenas emphasizing the significance of the number nine in spiritual observance.

Novenas are characterized by their structure, intentionality, and persistence. They typically involve praying specific prayers or devotions daily for nine consecutive days, often centered around a particular theme, saint, or event. The prayers may include invocations, scriptural passages, reflections, and petitions. Some novenas also incorporate fasting, acts of charity, or other spiritual practices as a means of deepening one's devotion and commitment.

The purpose of a novena varies depending on the focus and intention behind it. Novenas may be prayed for various reasons, such as seeking divine intervention, expressing gratitude, seeking guidance, seeking healing or consolation, or deepening one's faith and spiritual growth. They provide a structured and dedicated time for individuals to bring their intentions, desires, and concerns before God and the intercessory power of the saints.

Novenas are often associated with specific saints, whose intercession is sought during the nine-day period. Each saint may be venerated for their particular virtues, patronages, or spiritual significance. Praying a novena to a specific saint allows individuals to connect with that saint, seeking their assistance and guidance in specific areas of life.

Throughout the nine days of a novena, individuals are encouraged to approach their prayers with faith, trust, and perseverance. The repetitive nature of the novena serves to deepen one's focus, intention, and spiritual receptivity. By committing to daily prayer for a sustained period, believers demonstrate their dedication and reliance on God's grace and the intercession of the saint.

Novenas can be prayed individually, within families, or as a community, with many churches and religious organizations offering communal novena services. The communal aspect fosters a sense of unity and shared devotion, creating a supportive and prayerful environment.

It is important to note that while novenas are a cherished spiritual practice, they are not magical formulas or guarantees of specific outcomes. Praying a novena is an expression of faith, surrendering one's intentions and desires to God's will and trusting in His wisdom and providence. The journey of a novena can be transformative, deepening one's relationship with God and the saints, and nurturing a spirit of openness to His divine plan.

In summary, novenas are a cherished and purposeful form of prayer that span nine consecutive days. They provide a structured and intentional means of seeking divine intervention, expressing devotion, deepening faith, and connecting with the intercessory power of the saints. Novenas offer believers an opportunity for focused prayer, reflection, and spiritual growth, fostering a deeper relationship with God and His beloved saints.

1.2 History and Significance

The history and significance of novenas can be traced back to early Christian practices and traditions. While the specific origins may be difficult to pinpoint, the practice of dedicating a period of nine days to focused prayer and devotion has deep roots in both Jewish and Christian traditions.

In the Jewish faith, it was customary to observe a period of mourning for the deceased that lasted for seven days, known as the "Shiva" period. This period of mourning involved daily prayer and reflection. When Christianity emerged, it inherited and adapted various practices from its Jewish roots, including the concept of a set period of prayer and reflection.

The early Christian Church, inspired by the events of Pentecost and the apostles' nine-day vigil in the upper room, began to adopt and develop the practice of novenas. This period of nine days became associated with waiting, preparation, and intense prayer in anticipation of significant events or feasts. The number nine, symbolizing completeness or fullness, held a particular significance.

Over time, novenas became associated with specific intentions, saints, or liturgical seasons. They were seen as a way to enter more deeply into the mysteries of faith and to seek the intercession of the saints. Novenas were often linked to major feasts or important moments in the liturgical calendar, providing an opportunity for the faithful to prepare spiritually and reflect on the significance of these events.

The development and popularity of novenas continued throughout the centuries. In the Middle Ages, they became an essential part of popular piety, allowing the laity to engage in a structured and accessible form of prayer outside of formal liturgical settings. Novenas provided a means for individuals to express their devotion, seek assistance, and deepen their faith through the intercession of the saints.

The significance of novenas lies in their ability to foster a deeper spiritual connection with God and the saints. By dedicating a specific period of time to intentional prayer, believers demonstrate their commitment and openness to God's grace. Novenas serve as a framework for focused reflection, supplication, and gratitude, helping individuals draw closer to God and seek the intercession of the saints in their lives.

Novenas also have a communal aspect, as they can be prayed together as families, communities, or religious congregations. This communal prayer strengthens bonds, creates a sense of shared devotion, and builds a supportive spiritual environment. Many churches and religious organizations offer communal novena services, enhancing the communal aspect of the practice.

Today, novenas continue to hold a significant place in Catholic devotion and popular piety. They are seen as a means of deepening one's faith, seeking guidance and intercession, expressing gratitude, and preparing for important feasts or events. Novenas provide a structured and accessible form of prayer that allows individuals to engage in a focused and intentional spiritual journey.

The history and significance of novenas can be traced back to early Christian practices, adapting elements from Jewish traditions. Novenas provide a dedicated period of prayer and reflection, allowing believers to seek intercession, deepen their faith, and prepare for significant feasts or events. They hold a communal aspect and serve as a framework for individuals to express their devotion, supplicate, and express gratitude. Novenas continue to be an important part of Catholic devotion and popular piety, nurturing a deeper spiritual connection with God and the saints.

1.3 Benefits of Praying a Novena

Praying a novena offers numerous benefits that contribute to one's spiritual growth, emotional well-being, and personal relationship with God and the saints. Here are some of the key benefits associated with this cherished practice:

1. Deepened Faith: Engaging in a novena requires a commitment to daily prayer and reflection over a sustained period. This consistent practice helps deepen one's faith as it encourages a regular connection with the divine. By immersing oneself in prayer and contemplation, individuals can develop a greater trust in God's presence and guidance in their lives.

2. Intensified Prayer Life: Novenas provide a structured and intentional framework for prayer. Through the repetition of prayers, reflection on specific themes or virtues, and consistent focus on intentions, individuals can enhance the depth and intensity of their prayer life. The sustained period of prayer promotes a more profound and meaningful connection with God.

3. Increased Patience and Perseverance: The nine-day duration of a novena encourages patience and perseverance. It teaches individuals the value of persisting in prayer, even when answers may not be immediately evident. By embracing the discipline of a novena, individuals develop virtues such as patience, trust, and perseverance that can extend beyond the prayer practice itself and positively impact other areas of life.

4. Strengthened Relationship with the Saints: Novenas often focus on specific saints, inviting believers to seek their intercession and guidance. Through consistent prayer and reflection on the lives and virtues of the saints, individuals can develop a deeper connection with these holy figures.

This bond fosters a sense of spiritual companionship and inspires individuals to emulate the saint's virtues in their own lives.

5. Gratitude and Recognition of Blessings: Novenas provide an opportunity to express gratitude and recognize the blessings received in life. Throughout the nine-day period, individuals are encouraged to reflect on the goodness and grace bestowed upon them. This practice cultivates an attitude of gratitude and fosters a deeper appreciation for God's presence and provision.

6. Clarity and Discernment: The focused nature of a novena can facilitate clarity and discernment in decision-making processes. By dedicating time to prayer, reflection, and seeking the intercession of the saints, individuals can gain insight and guidance regarding important life choices or challenges they may be facing. Novenas offer a space for seeking divine wisdom and direction.

7. Sense of Community and Support: Novenas can be prayed individually or in community settings, fostering a sense of shared devotion and support. Engaging in a novena together with family, friends, or fellow believers creates a supportive environment where individuals can pray for one another's intentions, share experiences, and encourage each other on their spiritual journeys.

8. Spiritual Renewal and Transformation: The immersive nature of a novena, with its focused prayers, reflections, and intentions, can lead to spiritual renewal and transformation. It offers an opportunity for individuals to draw closer to God, deepen their relationship with Him, and experience personal growth and transformation. Novenas invite believers to open their hearts to God's grace and embrace His transformative power.

In summary, praying a novena yields a range of benefits, including deepened faith, intensified prayer life, increased patience and perseverance, strengthened relationships with the saints, gratitude and recognition of blessings, clarity and discernment, a sense of community and support, and spiritual renewal and transformation. By engaging in this cherished practice, individuals can experience profound growth and nourishment in their spiritual lives.

Chapter Two

St. Anne: A Saintly Figure

2.1 Life and Background of St. Anne

The life and background of St. Anne, the mother of the Virgin Mary and the grandmother of Jesus Christ, are not extensively documented in the Bible. However, certain traditions and apocryphal writings provide some insights into her story and significance within Christian tradition.

St. Anne's name is believed to be of Hebrew origin, meaning "grace" or "favor." According to ancient traditions, she was born in Bethlehem and was part of the lineage of King David. She belonged to the tribe of Levi, known for its association with the priesthood.

Anne married Joachim, a devout and righteous man from Nazareth. Together, they lived a life of deep faith and devotion to God. However, they faced the sorrow and disappointment of being childless for many years, which was regarded as a great burden and social stigma at the time.

In the apocryphal Gospel of James, an early Christian writing, the miraculous conception of St. Anne is described. It is said that in her old age, Anne received a vision from an angel who told her that she would conceive a child. In response to this divine message, Anne and Joachim dedicated themselves to fasting, prayer, and acts of charity, seeking God's favor and the fulfillment of the angel's prophecy.

God, in His providence, heard Anne's prayers, and she conceived a child. This conception was seen as a miraculous event, as Anne was thought to be barren. The child she conceived would grow up to be Mary, who became the mother of Jesus Christ.

As the mother of Mary, St. Anne played a significant role in salvation history. She is considered a figure of great importance and veneration within Christian tradition. While the Bible does not provide extensive details about her life, St. Anne's role as the mother of the mother of God has led to her being honored and revered as a symbol of faith, grace, and maternal love.

St. Anne's significance extends beyond her role as the mother of Mary. As the grandmother of Jesus, she holds a unique place in the lineage of Christ.

Her descendants, including Jesus' earthly father Joseph, were part of the royal line of David, fulfilling the Messianic prophecies of the Old Testament.

Throughout history, St. Anne has been venerated as a powerful intercessor and a source of maternal love and protection. She is often invoked for assistance in matters related to motherhood, fertility, childbirth, family life, and homemaking. Many churches and shrines around the world are dedicated to her, attracting pilgrims and devotees seeking her intercession and guidance.

While the biblical accounts of St. Anne's life are limited, her significance within Christian tradition and devotion remains profound. She is recognized as a model of faith, grace, and maternal love, inspiring believers to embrace these virtues in their own lives and seek her intercession in their prayers and petitions.

2.2 Role in Christian Tradition

St. Anne holds a significant role in Christian tradition, particularly within Catholicism, and has been revered as a saintly figure for centuries. Her role as the mother of the Virgin Mary and the grandmother of Jesus Christ has bestowed upon her a special place in the hearts of believers and in the unfolding of salvation history.

1. Maternal Lineage: St. Anne's most prominent role is as the mother of Mary. According to Christian tradition, Anne's miraculous conception of Mary, despite being previously barren, is seen as a divine intervention and a sign of God's favor. This extraordinary event elevated Anne's status and emphasized the special role she played in bringing forth the one who would become the Mother of God.

2. Grandmother of Jesus: As the grandmother of Jesus, St. Anne is seen as having a direct familial connection to the Son of God. This lineage holds great significance as it fulfills the prophecies of the Old Testament regarding the Messiah's descent from the line of David. St. Anne's role as Jesus' grandmother underscores her importance in the genealogy and historical context of Jesus' earthly lineage.

3. Exemplar of Virtues: St. Anne is revered as a model of various virtues that Christians seek to emulate. Her unwavering faith, patient endurance, humility, love, and strength are qualities that believers aspire to incorporate into their own lives. She is seen as a source of inspiration and a guide for cultivating these virtues and living a life that is pleasing to God.

4. Patroness and Intercessor: St. Anne is recognized as a powerful intercessor, and believers turn to her in prayer, seeking her help, guidance, and intercession before God. She is considered the patroness of numerous causes and groups, including mothers, women in labor, grandparents

homemakers, cabinetmakers, and miners, among others. Her intercessory role is seen as a means of seeking divine assistance and blessings in specific areas of life.

5. Devotional Practices: Throughout history, various devotions and customs have emerged around St. Anne. Pilgrimages to her shrines, prayers, novenas, and other forms of veneration are common expressions of devotion to her. Many churches, particularly those dedicated to St. Anne, hold special feasts and celebrations in her honor. These devotional practices serve to deepen the faithful's connection with St. Anne and their reliance on her intercession.

6. Representation of God's Plan: St. Anne's role in the life of Mary and in the genealogy of Jesus is seen as part of God's divine plan for salvation. Her presence in the Gospel narratives emphasizes the continuity and fulfillment of the Old Testament prophecies. St. Anne's inclusion in the scriptural accounts affirms the significance of familial connections, God's providential care, and the importance of the human lineage in the Incarnation.

St. Anne's role in Christian tradition goes beyond her historical significance as the mother and grandmother of Jesus. She is revered as a model of faith and virtue, a powerful intercessor, and a symbol of God's divine plan. Believers turn to St. Anne for guidance, support, and the assurance of her maternal care, recognizing her as a cherished saint within the tapestry of Christian devotion.

2.3 Patronages and Devotions

St. Anne is recognized as the patroness of various causes, groups, and professions. Throughout history, believers have sought her intercession and invoked her name for specific intentions. Additionally, numerous devotions and customs have emerged around St. Anne, providing ways for the faithful to express their devotion and seek her assistance. Here are some of the notable patronages and devotions associated with St. Anne:

1. Mothers and Women in Labor: St. Anne is widely regarded as the patroness of mothers, expectant mothers, and women in labor. Many women turn to her for support and intercession during pregnancy, childbirth, and motherhood. St. Anne's maternal role in the life of Mary and her understanding of the joys and challenges of motherhood make her a comforting and guiding figure for women in these circumstances.

2. Grandparents: As the grandmother of Jesus, St. Anne is also recognized as the patroness of grandparents. Her example as a faithful and nurturing grandmother inspires and guides grandparents in their important role within families. St. Anne's intercession is sought for the well-being, guidance, and spiritual growth of grandchildren.

3. Homemakers and Housewives: St. Anne is seen as a patroness of homemakers and housewives, honoring her domestic role as a wife and mother. Many women turn to her for guidance, strength, and inspiration in their daily tasks and responsibilities within the home. St. Anne's example of love, care, and devotion in creating a nurturing environment resonates with those in these roles.

4. Cabinetmakers and Craftsmen: St. Anne is traditionally regarded as the patroness of cabinetmakers and craftsmen. This association may stem from legends and depictions of her husband, Joachim, being skilled in woodworking. St. Anne's intercession is sought for those involved in these professions, seeking guidance, inspiration, and skill in their work.

5. Miners: St. Anne is recognized as the patroness of miners. This patronage can be traced back to historical associations of her intercession in protecting miners from harm and ensuring their safety while working in the challenging conditions of mines. Miners turn to St. Anne for her watchful care and protection in their dangerous occupation.

Devotions to St. Anne often include prayers, novenas, and pilgrimages to her shrines and holy sites. The Novena to St. Anne is a popular practice, consisting of nine consecutive days of prayer and reflection. It provides a structured framework for seeking St. Anne's intercession and deepening one's spiritual connection with her.

Pilgrimages to sites associated with St. Anne, such as the Basilica of Sainte-Anne-de-Beaupré in Quebec, Canada, or the Santuario di Sant'Anna in Ischia, Italy, are also common devotional practices. These pilgrimages offer opportunities for believers to seek St. Anne's intercession, express their devotion, and participate in religious ceremonies and rituals dedicated to her.

Various prayers, such as the Prayer to St. Anne or the Chaplet of St. Anne, are recited to seek her assistance and guidance. These prayers express gratitude, invoke her intercession, and seek blessings in specific areas of life, such as motherhood, family life, or personal intentions.

St. Anne is recognized as the patroness of mothers, women in labor, grandparents, homemakers, cabinetmakers, and miners, among other groups. Devotions to St. Anne include prayers, novenas, pilgrimages, and specific customs associated with seeking her intercession. Her patronages and devotions offer solace, guidance, and spiritual support to individuals in various walks of life, fostering a deeper connection with this beloved saint.

Chapter Three

Praying the Novena to St. Anne

3.1 Preparation and Setting Intentions

Preparing for and setting intentions for a novena to St. Anne can enhance the depth and focus of your prayer journey. Taking the time to prepare your heart and mind before beginning the novena can contribute to a more meaningful and transformative experience. Here are some suggestions for preparation and setting intentions:

1. Find a Sacred Space: Choose a quiet and peaceful place where you can pray without distractions. Create a sacred space that helps you feel connected to God and St. Anne. This can include items like a statue or image of St. Anne, a candle, a Bible, or other symbols that hold personal significance for you.

. Educate Yourself: Learn more about St. Anne's life, virtues, and significance within Christian tradition. Read about her in the Bible and explore reputable resources that provide insights into her story and the devotion surrounding her. This knowledge will deepen your understanding and appreciation of St. Anne as you embark on the novena.

3. Reflect on Your Intentions: Take time to reflect on your intentions for the novena. What specific areas of your life do you want to bring before God and seek St. Anne's intercession for? Are there particular challenges, needs, or desires that you want to lift up in prayer? Write down your intentions, allowing yourself to be honest and vulnerable before God.

4. Set Clear and Specific Intentions: While it is essential to bring all aspects of your life before God, consider setting clear and specific intentions for the novena. This helps focus your prayers and invites you to be intentional in seeking St. Anne's intercession for particular areas of your life. Be specific about the outcomes you desire and the areas where you need guidance, healing, or blessings.

5. Openness to God's Will: As you set your intentions, remember to approach them with an attitude of openness and surrender to God's will. While it is natural to have specific desires and hopes, trust that God know what is best for you. Offer your intentions to God, expressing you willingness to accept His plan and guidance, even if it may differ from what you initially expect or desire.

6. Seek St. Anne's Intercession: Pray to St. Anne, asking for her guidance and intercession as you embark on the novena. Express your trust in her maternal care and her ability to bring your intentions before God. Seek her help in aligning your intentions with God's will and ask her to accompany you on this spiritual journey.

7. Gather Prayers and Resources: Collect the prayers, reflections, and resources you will need for the novena. These can include traditional prayers to St. Anne, specific novena prayers, or other devotions associated with her. Having these resources readily available will facilitate your daily prayer practice and help you stay focused throughout the nine days.

Remember that preparation and setting intentions are personal and unique to each individual. Tailor these suggestions to align with your own spiritual practices and beliefs. The key is to approach the novena with a sincere and open heart, ready to engage in deep prayer, reflection, and seeking the intercession of St. Anne for your intentions.

3.2 The Nine-Day Prayer Structure

The Novena to St. Anne follows a nine-day prayer structure, with each day dedicated to a specific theme, virtue, or aspect of St. Anne's life. This structure provides a framework for focused prayer, reflection, and meditation, allowing for a deep exploration of St. Anne's example and seeking her intercession. While specific prayers and reflections may vary, the following is a suggested outline for the nine days of the novena:

Day 1: Introduction and Invocation

- Begin by invoking St. Anne's intercession and inviting her presence during the novena.

- Reflect on St. Anne's significance and her role as the mother of Mary and the grandmother of Jesus.

Day 2: Faith and Trust

- Reflect on St. Anne's unwavering faith and trust in God.

- Pray for an increase in your own faith and trust in God's providence and guidance.

Day 3: Patience and Endurance

- Contemplate St. Anne's patient waiting for the fulfillment of God's promises.

- Pray for the virtue of patience and the ability to endure challenges with grace and perseverance.

Day 4: Hope and Expectation

- Reflect on St. Anne's hopeful anticipation of God's blessings.

- Pray for a deep and abiding hope in God's promises and the grace to live with joyful expectation.

Day 5: Love and Compassion

- Meditate on St. Anne's love and compassion as a mother and grandmother.
- Pray for a heart filled with love and compassion, particularly towards your family and those in need.

Day 6: Humility and Surrender

- Reflect on St. Anne's humility in accepting God's plan for her life.
- Pray for the virtue of humility and the ability to surrender your own will to God's will.

Day 7: Strength and Courage

- Contemplate St. Anne's strength and courage in facing life's challenges.
- Pray for inner strength and courage to navigate difficulties and embrace God's call.

Day 8: Gratitude and Thanksgiving

- Reflect on St. Anne's gratitude for God's blessings in her life.
- Offer prayers of gratitude and thanksgiving for the blessings you have received.

Day 9: Renewal and Petitions

- Reflect on the lessons learned from St. Anne's life and virtues.

- Offer your specific intentions and petitions to St. Anne, seeking her intercession for your needs.

In each daily prayer, incorporate reflections, readings from Scripture, and specific prayers associated with the theme of the day. You may choose to recite traditional prayers to St. Anne or compose your own heartfelt prayers. Use this structure as a guide, but feel free to adapt and personalize the novena to align with your own spirituality and devotional practices.

It is important to always approach each day with openness, receptivity, and a sincere desire to draw closer to St. Anne and God through prayer and reflection. Allow the novena to be a transformative journey of faith, seeking St. Anne's intercession and guidance for your intentions and deepening your spiritual connection with this beloved saint.

3.3 Practices and Customs during the Novena

During the Novena to St. Anne, there are various practices and customs that can enrich your experience and deepen your devotion. These practices help create a sacred atmosphere and foster a more focused and intentional prayer journey. Here are some suggested practices and customs to consider during the novena:

1. Daily Prayer: Set aside a specific time each day to engage in prayer. Dedicate this time solely to prayer and reflection, free from distractions. Use prayers specifically associated with St. Anne, such as the Prayer to St. Anne or the Chaplet of St. Anne. You can also incorporate other prayers and devotions that resonate with you and align with the themes of the novena.

2. Reflection and Meditation: Allocate time for quiet reflection and meditation during the novena. Consider reflecting on St. Anne's virtues, her role in salvation history, and her example of faith and love. Meditate on specific Scripture passages that relate to the daily theme or on passages that highlight St. Anne's significance. Allow these moments of reflection to deepen your understanding and connection with St. Anne.

3. Pilgrimage or Visit: If possible, consider visiting a shrine or church dedicated to St. Anne during the novena. Many places around the world are dedicated to St. Anne, such as the Basilica of Sainte-Anne-de-Beaupré in Quebec, Canada, or the Santuario di Sant'Anna in Ischia, Italy. Pilgrimages to these holy sites can provide a unique opportunity to offer your prayers, participate in liturgical celebrations, and experience the presence of St. Anne in a special way.

. Lighting Candles: Light a candle as a symbol of your prayers and intentions. Place the candle in your sacred space and keep it burning during your daily prayer time. The flickering flame can serve as a visual reminder of your devotion and the light of faith.

5. Offering Flowers: St. Anne is often associated with flowers, particularly lilies. Consider placing flowers, especially lilies or other favorites, in your sacred space as an offering and a symbol of your devotion. You can also offer a bouquet of flowers at a shrine or church dedicated to St. Anne, if possible.

6. Acts of Charity: Perform acts of charity and kindness during the novena as a way to honor St. Anne's example of love and compassion. Reach out to those in need, lend a helping hand, or make a donation to a charitable organization. By embodying St. Anne's virtues through acts of service, you align your actions with your prayers.

7. Journaling: Keep a journal to record your reflections, prayers, and experiences during the novena. Write down any insights, inspirations, or answers to prayers that you receive. Journaling allows you to capture your thoughts and emotions, providing a record of your spiritual journey and serving as a reminder of God's presence and St. Anne's intercession.

8. Fasting or Abstinence: Consider incorporating fasting or abstinence into your novena practice, if appropriate and in consultation with your spiritual

advisor or religious traditions. Fasting can be done in various forms, such as abstaining from certain foods or activities. It can be a way to offer sacrifice and deepen your prayer experience.

Remember that these practices and customs are suggestions, and you can adapt them to suit your own personal preferences and spiritual traditions. The goal is to create an atmosphere of devotion, focus, and reverence as you journey through the novena, seeking St. Anne's intercession and deepening your connection with her and with God.

Day 1 - The Faith of St. Anne

Reflections on St. Anne's Faith

St. Anne's faith is a shining example for believers, as she demonstrated unwavering trust and devotion to God throughout her life. Her steadfast faith serves as an inspiration and a model for us to deepen our own faith. Reflecting on St. Anne's faith can encourage us to cultivate similar qualities in our spiritual journey. Here are some key aspects to consider:

1. Trust in God's Timing: St. Anne's faith was evident in her patient trust in God's timing and plan. Despite years of barrenness, she never lost hope or abandoned her faith. Instead, she continued to pray and remain faithful, believing that God's promises would be fulfilled. This teaches us the importance of trusting in God's timing, even when our own desires and plans are not immediately realized. St. Anne's example encourages us to persevere in faith, knowing that God's timing is perfect.

2. Humble Acceptance of God's Will: St. Anne's faith was characterized by humble acceptance of God's will in her life. She embraced her role as the mother of Mary and the grandmother of Jesus with humility and obedience. St. Anne recognized that her purpose was aligned with God's plan, and she embraced it wholeheartedly. This challenges us to reflect on our own willingness to accept God's will in our lives, even when it may diverge from our own desires or expectations. St. Anne's faith calls us to surrender our own wills and trust in God's providence.

3. Deep Prayer and Devotion: St. Anne's faith was nurtured through a life of deep prayer and devotion. She dedicated herself to seeking God's presence and guidance through prayer, fasting, and acts of charity. St. Anne's prayer life serves as a reminder of the importance of cultivating a vibrant and intimate relationship with God through regular prayer and spiritual practices. Her example encourages us to prioritize prayer in our own lives and to develop a close bond with God through daily communion with Him.

4. Firm Foundation in Scripture: St. Anne's faith was rooted in the rich traditions and teachings of the Scriptures. As a faithful Jewish woman, she would have been well-versed in the Scriptures and the promises of God. St. Anne's faith challenges us to deepen our knowledge and understanding of God's Word, allowing it to form the foundation of our faith. By immersing

ourselves in Scripture, we can discover the truths and promises of God that sustain our faith and guide our lives.

5. Intercession and Intergenerational Faith: St. Anne's faith extended beyond her own life and had a profound impact on future generations. Her intercession and influence on the life of her daughter, Mary, played a significant role in salvation history. St. Anne's faith inspires us to consider our own influence on the faith of those around us, particularly our children and grandchildren. We are called to intercede for them, nurture their faith, and pass on the legacy of faith to future generations.

Reflecting on St. Anne's faith invites us to examine our own faith and to strive for a deeper and more authentic relationship with God. Her unwavering trust in God's timing, humble acceptance of His will, commitment to prayer, foundation in Scripture, and intergenerational faith all serve as powerful lessons for us on our own faith journey. As we contemplate St. Anne's faith, may we be inspired to emulate her virtues and grow in our own faith and devotion to God.

Prayers for the First Day

Dear St. Anne,

You who lived a life of faith and trust in God,

I come before you seeking your intercession.

You believed in God's promises and remained steadfast,

Even in times of uncertainty and waiting.

I humbly ask for your help in strengthening my faith,

For there are moments when doubt and fear creep in.

Grant me the grace to trust in God's plan for my life,

To surrender my will to His and embrace His timing.

St. Anne, you knew the power of prayer,

And you lived a life of deep devotion to God.

Please pray for me, that I may develop a strong and unwavering faith,

That I may always seek God's will and walk in His ways.

Help me to find inspiration in your example,

To cultivate a life of prayer, Scripture study, and acts of charity.

May my faith grow each day, anchored in God's Word,

And may it be a light that shines in the darkness.

St. Anne, grandmother of Jesus and mother of Mary,

Intercede for me before the throne of God.

Obtain for me the grace to trust in Him completely,

To believe in His love, goodness, and faithfulness.

In your loving care, guide me closer to God,

That I may live with a faith that is strong and unshakable.

St. Anne, pray for me and all who seek to deepen their faith,

That we may know the joy and peace that come from trusting in God alone.

Amen.

May this prayer to St. Anne for faith inspire and strengthen your trust in God's providence and goodness. Place your hopes and intentions before her, and ask for her powerful intercession as you strive to grow in faith and deepen your relationship with God.

Day 2 - The Patience of St. Anne

Reflections on St. Anne's Patience

St. Anne's patience is a remarkable virtue that shines through her life and serves as an inspiration for believers. Her example of enduring with grace and trust in God's timing offers valuable lessons for us to reflect upon. Here are some reflections on St. Anne's patience:

1. Trusting in God's Timing: St. Anne's life teaches us the importance of trusting in God's timing, even when it seems like our prayers are not immediately answered. Despite years of barrenness, St. Anne did not lose hope or become discouraged. Instead, she placed her trust in God's plan and continued to seek His guidance through prayer and faith. Her patience reminds us that God's timing is perfect, and He works all things for our good according to His divine wisdom.

2. Enduring Difficulties with Grace: St. Anne's patience was not passive resignation, but rather a strength that enabled her to endure difficulties with grace. Despite societal pressures and the personal pain of being childless,

she remained steadfast in her faith and remained committed to living a virtuous life. Her example encourages us to face our own challenges with patience, perseverance, and a spirit of grace. By trusting in God's plan and seeking His strength, we can navigate difficult circumstances with hope and dignity.

3. Nurturing Hope in the Midst of Waiting: St. Anne's patience was intertwined with hope. Despite the long years of waiting for a child, she did not allow despair to overcome her. Instead, she nurtured a hopeful expectation that God would fulfill His promises. Her steadfast hope teaches us to cultivate a similar attitude in our own lives. By placing our hope in God's faithfulness and goodness, we can endure seasons of waiting with a sense of anticipation and trust.

4. Embracing the Journey of Growth: St. Anne's patience was not solely about waiting for a desired outcome; it also involved personal growth and spiritual development. During the years of waiting, she deepened her relationship with God, honed her virtues, and became a woman of faith and grace. Her patience reminds us that the journey itself is an opportunity for growth and transformation. It invites us to embrace the process, knowing that God is working within us and preparing us for His purposes.

5. Surrendering to God's Will: St. Anne's patience was marked by surrendering to God's will. She accepted that her plans and desires might

differ from God's plan, and she embraced His will with humility and trust. Her example challenges us to surrender our own wills and desires to God, acknowledging that His plan is ultimately for our best. By embracing His will, we open ourselves to His guidance and the fulfillment of His purposes in our lives.

Reflecting on St. Anne's patience encourages us to cultivate a similar virtue in our own lives. Through trust in God's timing, grace in the face of difficulties, nurturing hope, embracing growth, and surrendering to His will, we can develop a patient spirit that allows us to navigate life's challenges with faith and perseverance. St. Anne's example reminds us that in patience, we can find strength, grace, and a deeper connection with God.

Prayers for the Second Day

O St. Anne,

You who exemplified the virtue of patience,

I come before you seeking your intercession.

You endured years of waiting and uncertainty,

Yet your faith remained steadfast and unwavering.

I humbly ask for your help in cultivating patience within me,

For there are times when I grow restless and anxious.

Grant me the grace to trust in God's timing and plan,

To surrender my own desires and embrace His will.

St. Anne, you knew the challenges of waiting,

And you bore them with grace and perseverance.

Please pray for me, that I may develop a patient spirit,

That I may learn to wait with hope and trust in God's providence.

Help me to find solace in prayer and reflection,

To seek God's guidance and strength during times of waiting.

May I remember that waiting is not idle time,

But an opportunity for growth, surrender, and deeper reliance on God.

St. Anne, grandmother of Jesus and mother of Mary,

Intercede for me before the throne of God.

Obtain for me the grace to cultivate patience in my life,

To trust in God's timing and surrender to His will.

In your loving care, guide me closer to God,

That I may live with patience, grace, and faith.

St. Anne, pray for me and all who seek to develop patience,

That we may embrace waiting as an opportunity for growth and deepening

our relationship with God.

Amen.

May this prayer to St. Anne for patience bring you comfort and inspiration as you seek to cultivate this virtue in your life. Place your hopes and intentions before her, and ask for her powerful intercession to help you develop a patient spirit rooted in trust and surrender to God's will.

Day 3 - The Hope of St. Anne

Reflections on St. Anne's Hope

St. Anne's hope is a profound virtue that serves as a beacon of light and inspiration for believers. Her unwavering trust in God's promises and her hopeful anticipation teach us important lessons about the power of hope in our own lives. Here are some reflections on St. Anne's hope:

1. Trusting in God's Promises: St. Anne's hope was firmly rooted in her trust in God's promises. Despite years of waiting for a child, she never lost faith in God's goodness and His faithfulness to His people. Her hope was not based on mere wishful thinking but on the assurance that God would fulfil His plans in His perfect timing. St. Anne's example encourages us to place our hope in God's promises, knowing that He is faithful to His Word.

2. Nurturing Expectation: St. Anne nurtured a hopeful expectation that God's blessings would be bestowed upon her. She did not allow discouragement or doubt to overshadow her hope. Instead, she continued t

pray and believe in God's plan for her life. Her hopeful anticipation challenges us to nurture a similar expectation in our own lives. We can cultivate hope by trusting in God's goodness, seeking His guidance, and actively seeking His will in our lives.

3. Embracing Waiting with Hope: St. Anne's hope was intertwined with waiting. She endured years of waiting for a child, yet she did not lose hope. Instead, she embraced the waiting period as an opportunity for growth and deepening her trust in God. St. Anne's example teaches us that hope is not passive but active. It allows us to embrace the present moment with anticipation, knowing that God is working behind the scenes and that His plans are unfolding.

4. Persevering in Prayer: St. Anne's hope was sustained through her perseverance in prayer. She did not give up but continued to lift her desires and intentions to God in prayer. Her example reminds us of the power of persistent and faithful prayer. By persevering in prayer, we can strengthen our hope, deepen our relationship with God, and align our desires with His will.

5. Finding Strength in God's Promises: St. Anne's hope was a source of strength and resilience. It enabled her to face the challenges of life with courage and determination. Her hope in God's promises gave her the strength to endure and persevere. St. Anne's example encourages us to find

strength in our own hope in God. In times of difficulty or uncertainty, we can draw on the hope that comes from trusting in His promises and knowing that He is with us.

Reflecting on St. Anne's hope reminds us of the power and significance of hope in our own lives. By trusting in God's promises, nurturing expectation, embracing waiting with hope, persevering in prayer, and finding strength in our hope in God, we can cultivate a hopeful spirit that sustains us through life's challenges. St. Anne's example encourages us to place our hope in God, knowing that He is faithful and that His plans for us are good.

Prayers for the Third Day

Dear St. Anne,

You who embraced hope in God's plan,

I come before you seeking your intercession.

You trusted in God's promises and remained hopeful,

Even in the face of uncertainty and waiting.

I humbly ask for your help in fostering hope within me,

For there are times when doubt and discouragement creep in.

Grant me the grace to trust in God's plan for my life,

To have unwavering hope in His goodness and faithfulness.

St. Anne, you knew the power of prayer and perseverance,

And you nurtured a hopeful anticipation of God's blessings.

Please pray for me, that I may cultivate a steadfast hope,

That I may find strength in God's promises and His loving plan.

Help me to surrender my fears and worries to God,

And to trust that He is working all things for my good.

May I have the courage to embrace the waiting with hope,

Knowing that God's timing is perfect and His plans are unfolding.

St. Anne, grandmother of Jesus and mother of Mary,

Intercede for me before the throne of God.

Obtain for me the grace to foster hope in His plan,

To trust that He has a purpose for my life and will guide me.

In your loving care, guide me closer to God,

That I may live with hope, faith, and joyful anticipation.

St. Anne, pray for me and all who seek hope in God's plan,

That we may be filled with confidence, peace, and trust in His providence.

Amen.

May this prayer to St. Anne for hope in God's plan bring comfort and strength to your heart as you place your hopes and intentions before her. Ask for her intercession and trust in her powerful prayers as you cultivate unwavering hope in God's goodness and loving plan for your life. May your hope be renewed, and may you find peace and joy in trusting in His providence.

Day 4 - The Love of St. Anne

Reflections on St. Anne's Love

St. Anne's love is a beautiful testament to the power of a mother's heart and serves as a profound example for all believers. Her love for God, her family, and humanity radiates through her life, teaching us valuable lessons about the transformative nature of love. Here are some reflections on St. Anne's love:

1. Love for God: St. Anne's love for God was at the core of her being. She lived her life in faithful devotion and deep reverence for God. Her love for God permeated every aspect of her existence, guiding her actions and decisions. St. Anne's example encourages us to cultivate a similar love for God, to seek a deep and intimate relationship with Him, and to make Him the center of our lives.

. Maternal Love: As the mother of Mary, St. Anne's love as a mother was profound. She nurtured and cared for her daughter, providing her with a loving and supportive environment. St. Anne's maternal love reminds us of the power and importance of a mother's role in shaping the lives of her children. Her example inspires us to love and care for our own children and to embrace the responsibility of nurturing their physical, emotional, and spiritual well-being.

3. Love for Humanity: St. Anne's love extended beyond her immediate family. She embraced a love for all humanity, recognizing the inherent dignity and worth of every person. Her love was inclusive and compassionate, reflecting the love of God for His creation. St. Anne's example challenges us to extend our love beyond our own circles and to embrace a love that encompasses all people, treating them with kindness, respect, and compassion.

4. Sacrificial Love: St. Anne's love was marked by selflessness and sacrifice. She embraced her role as a mother and grandmother with dedication and devotion, putting the needs of her loved ones before her own. St. Anne's sacrificial love teaches us that genuine love requires sacrifice putting others' well-being and happiness above our own desires and comforts. Her example encourages us to love sacrificially, following the example of Christ's love for us.

5. Love as a Healing Force: St. Anne's love had a transformative power. Her love and care provided a healing presence in the lives of those she encountered. St. Anne's love reminds us of the potential impact our love can

have on others. It inspires us to extend love and compassion to those who are hurting, marginalized, or in need. Her example calls us to be instruments of God's love in the world, offering healing and restoration through acts of kindness, understanding, and forgiveness.

Reflecting on St. Anne's love encourages us to cultivate a similar love in our own lives. By embracing love for God, nurturing maternal love, extending love to all humanity, practicing sacrificial love, and recognizing the healing power of love, we can make a positive difference in the lives of those around us. St. Anne's example invites us to let love be the guiding force in our relationships, allowing it to transform us and the world around us.

Prayers for the Fourth Day

Our loving St. Anne,

You who embodied love in its purest form,

I come before you seeking your intercession.

You loved God, your family, and all humanity,

Radiating love through your words and actions.

I humbly ask for your help in cultivating love within me,

For there are times when my heart feels closed or distant.

Grant me the grace to love as you did,

To love God with all my heart and to love my neighbors as myself.

St. Anne, you knew the transformative power of love,

And your maternal love was a reflection of God's love.

Please pray for me, that I may grow in love,

That I may embrace a love that is selfless, compassionate, and inclusive.

Help me to extend love to all those I encounter,

To treat them with kindness, respect, and understanding.

May I embrace sacrificial love, putting others' needs before my own,

And may my love be a healing balm for those who are hurting.

St. Anne, grandmother of Jesus and mother of Mary,

Intercede for me before the throne of God.

Obtain for me the grace to love as you did,

To love God wholeheartedly and to love my neighbors unconditionally.

In your loving care, guide me closer to God,

That I may be filled with His love and radiate it to others.

St. Anne, pray for me and all who seek to cultivate love,

That we may be instruments of God's love in the world.

Amen.

May this prayer to St. Anne for love inspire and guide you as you seek to cultivate love in your life. Place your hopes and intentions before her, and ask for her intercession to help you grow in love for God, for your family, and for all humanity. May her powerful prayers and example of love lead you to a deeper understanding of God's love and a greater capacity to love others.

Day 5 - The Humility of St. Anne

Reflections on St. Anne's Humility

St. Anne's humility shines as a radiant virtue and offers profound lessons for all believers. Her humble spirit and willingness to surrender to God's will serve as an example for us to reflect upon. Here are some reflections on St. Anne's humility:

1. Acceptance of God's Plan: St. Anne's humility was demonstrated through her acceptance of God's plan for her life. Despite her own desires and expectations, she surrendered to God's will, trusting in His wisdom and guidance. Her example challenges us to examine our own hearts and embrace God's plan for our lives, even if it differs from our own desires or expectations. St. Anne's humility teaches us to align our will with God's will and to find peace and fulfillment in following His path.

2. Recognition of God's Greatness: St. Anne's humility was rooted in her recognition of God's greatness and her dependence on Him. She acknowledged her own limitations and understood that all good things come

from God. St. Anne's humility prompts us to acknowledge our own dependence on God and to approach Him with reverence and awe. It reminds us that true greatness lies in recognizing God's supremacy and submitting ourselves to His divine authority.

3. Service to Others: St. Anne's humility was exemplified through her acts of service and selflessness. As a mother and grandmother, she dedicated herself to nurturing and caring for her family. Her humility allowed her to put others' needs before her own, to serve with love and compassion. St. Anne's humility challenges us to embrace a similar spirit of service, to humbly use our gifts and resources for the well-being of others, and to seek opportunities to serve with a genuine and selfless heart.

4. Gratitude and Praise: St. Anne's humility was expressed through her gratitude and praise for God's blessings. She recognized that all good things come from God's hand and humbly acknowledged His goodness in her life. St. Anne's humility teaches us to cultivate a spirit of gratitude and praise, to humbly recognize and acknowledge God's blessings in our own lives. It invites us to develop an attitude of thankfulness and to offer our praises to God, recognizing that everything we have is a gift from Him.

. Embracing a Lowly Status: St. Anne's humility is reflected in her acceptance of a lowly status in society. She did not seek recognition or honor but embraced her role as a faithful servant of God. St. Anne's humility challenges us to embrace our own lowly status before God, to let go of pride and worldly ambitions, and to humbly submit ourselves to God's will. It invites us to find joy and contentment in fulfilling the roles and responsibilities that God has entrusted to us.

Reflecting on St. Anne's humility encourages us to cultivate a similar humility in our own lives. By accepting God's plan, recognizing His greatness, serving others, expressing gratitude and praise, and embracing a lowly status, we can grow in humility and deepen our relationship with God. St. Anne's example teaches us that true greatness lies in humble surrender to God's will and in the selfless service of others.

Prayers for the Fifth Day

O St. Anne,

You who embodied humility in its purest form,

I come before you seeking your intercession.

You embraced God's plan with humility and surrender,

Setting an example of true greatness in your life.

I humbly ask for your help in cultivating humility within me,

For there are times when pride and self-centeredness cloud my heart.

Grant me the grace to embrace humility,

To recognize my limitations and to surrender to God's will.

St. Anne, you knew the beauty of accepting God's plan,

And you lived a life of selfless service and love.

Please pray for me, that I may grow in humility,

That I may let go of pride and embrace a spirit of selflessness.

Help me to recognize God's greatness and authority,

To acknowledge His blessings with gratitude and praise.

May I serve others with a humble and loving heart,

Putting their needs before my own and reflecting Christ's love.

St. Anne, grandmother of Jesus and mother of Mary,

Intercede for me before the throne of God.

Obtain for me the grace to cultivate humility,

To let go of worldly ambitions and to embrace God's plan for my life.

In your loving care, guide me closer to God,

That I may learn from your example and live with humility.

St. Anne, pray for me and all who seek to cultivate humility,

That we may find true greatness in surrendering to God's will.

Amen.

May this prayer to St. Anne for humility inspire and guide you as you seek to cultivate this virtue in your life. Place your hopes and intentions before her, and ask for her intercession to help you embrace humility, surrender to God's will, and serve others with a selfless heart. May her powerful prayers and example of humility lead you to a deeper understanding of true greatness and a closer relationship with God.

Day 6 - The Strength of St. Anne

Reflections on St. Anne's Strength

S t. Anne's strength serves as an inspiring example of resilience, courage, and steadfastness. Her unwavering faith and determination in the face of challenges offer valuable insights for reflection. Here are some reflections on St. Anne's strength:

1. Trusting in God's Plan: St. Anne's strength was rooted in her trust in God's plan. Despite the difficulties and uncertainties she faced, she held firm in her faith, believing that God's will would be fulfilled. Her example encourages us to trust in God's providence and to find strength in the knowledge that He works all things for our good. St. Anne's strength reminds us that relying on God's plan and purpose can empower us to face any challenge with confidence.

2. Enduring Trials with Grace: St. Anne's strength enabled her to endure trials with grace and dignity. From the longing for a child to societal pressures and the challenges of motherhood, she faced numerous obstacles.

Yet, she did not succumb to despair or lose sight of her faith. Instead, she embraced her trials with grace, relying on God's strength to persevere. St. Anne's example teaches us that true strength is not found in avoiding challenges but in facing them with faith and resilience.

3. Embracing Motherhood: St. Anne's strength as a mother shines through her nurturing and caring spirit. She embraced the responsibilities of motherhood with love and devotion, raising Mary to become the mother of Jesus. St. Anne's strength as a mother inspires us to reflect on the transformative power of a mother's love and the strength that can be found in selflessly caring for others. Her example challenges us to embrace our own roles and responsibilities with strength and love.

4. Deepening Faith through Prayer: St. Anne's strength was fortified through her deep and consistent prayer life. She sought solace, guidance, and strength from God through prayer, which allowed her to face challenges with renewed faith and courage. St. Anne's example reminds us of the importance of cultivating a vibrant prayer life to draw strength from God. Through prayer, we can find the inner strength needed to navigate life's trials and to grow in our relationship with God.

5. Trusting in God's Providence: St. Anne's strength came from her trust in God's providence. She believed that God would provide for her and her family, even in the face of adversity. St. Anne's trust in God's provision

challenges us to let go of worry and fear, placing our trust in His loving care. Her example encourages us to rely on God's strength and guidance, knowing that He will sustain us and provide for our needs.

Reflecting on St. Anne's strength invites us to examine our own lives and to draw inspiration from her example. By trusting in God's plan, enduring trials with grace, embracing our roles with love, deepening our faith through prayer, and trusting in God's providence, we can cultivate a similar strength within ourselves. St. Anne's strength reminds us that we are not alone in our struggles, for God is with us, providing the strength we need to overcome obstacles and grow in our faith.

Prayers for the Sixth Day

Dear St. Anne,

You who embodied strength and resilience,

  come before you seeking your intercession.

You faced challenges with unwavering faith,

  Drawing strength from God in every trial.

  humbly ask for your help in finding strength within me,

  or there are times when I feel weak and overwhelmed.

Grant me the grace to embrace your example of strength,

o rely on God's power and find courage in His presence.

St. Anne, you trusted in God's plan and providence,

Even when faced with difficulties and uncertainties.

Please pray for me, that I may find strength in trusting Him,

That I may face my challenges with courage and resilience.

Help me to endure trials with grace and dignity,

Knowing that God's strength is made perfect in weakness.

May I rely on His power and find solace in His love,

Finding the strength to persevere through every obstacle.

St. Anne, grandmother of Jesus and mother of Mary,

Intercede for me before the throne of God.

Obtain for me the grace to find strength in His presence,

To trust in His plan and to draw courage from His promises.

In your loving care, guide me closer to God,

That I may find renewed strength in His presence.

St. Anne, pray for me and all who seek strength,

That we may rely on God's power and face challenges with unwaverin
faith.

Amen.

May this prayer to St. Anne for strength inspire and uplift you as you face challenges in your life. Place your hopes and intentions before her, and ask for her intercession to help you find strength in God's presence. May her powerful prayers and example of resilience guide you to rely on God's power, find courage in His promises, and face every obstacle with unwavering faith.

Day 7 - The Guidance of St. Anne

Reflections on St. Anne's Guidance

St. Anne's guidance serves as a source of wisdom and inspiration for believers, offering valuable insights for navigating life's journey. Her guidance, rooted in faith and love, provides us with reflections to consider. Here are some reflections on St. Anne's guidance:

1. Trusting in God's Providence: St. Anne's guidance was grounded in her trust in God's providence. She relied on God's wisdom and guidance, seeking His will in her life. Her example challenges us to trust in God's guidance, even when the path may seem uncertain or unclear. St. Anne's guidance reminds us to surrender our plans to God, seeking His direction and trusting that He will lead us on the right path.

2. Embracing Prayer and Reflection: St. Anne's guidance was nurtured through prayer and reflection. She sought God's guidance through deep communion with Him, finding solace and wisdom in His presence. St. Anne's example encourages us to cultivate a vibrant prayer life and to set

aside time for reflection, allowing us to hear God's gentle voice and receive His guidance. Through prayer and reflection, we can seek clarity and discernment in the choices we face.

3. Nurturing a Spirit of Discernment: St. Anne's guidance involved a spirit of discernment. She carefully considered the choices before her, seeking to align her decisions with God's will. Her example challenges us to cultivate a similar spirit of discernment, seeking God's guidance and wisdom in our own lives. St. Anne's guidance reminds us to pause, pray, and seek God's perspective before making important decisions, trusting that He will illuminate the path before us.

4. Embracing Motherly Guidance: As the mother of Mary, St. Anne's guidance extended to nurturing and supporting her daughter. Her motherly guidance served as a source of wisdom and love, providing a steady hand and a caring heart. St. Anne's example encourages us to embrace a similar role in guiding and supporting those entrusted to our care. Whether as parents, mentors, or friends, we can offer guidance rooted in love, wisdom, and compassion.

5. Offering Guidance through Example: St. Anne's guidance was not limited to words; she exemplified her teachings through her own life. Her virtuous and faith-filled life served as a powerful form of guidance for others. St. Anne's example challenges us to be living examples of the values and

principles we wish to guide others with. Through our actions and attitudes, we can offer guidance and inspire others to walk the path of faith and love.

Reflecting on St. Anne's guidance encourages us to seek God's wisdom, trust in His providence, and offer guidance to others rooted in love and faith. Her example invites us to cultivate a spirit of discernment, to seek God's guidance through prayer and reflection, and to embrace our roles as guides and mentors. By following St. Anne's example, we can navigate life's challenges with wisdom, faith, and love, trusting in God's guidance every step of the way.

Prayers for the Seventh Day

Dear St. Anne,

You who offered guidance and wisdom,

I come before you seeking your intercession.

You trusted in God's providence and sought His guidance,

Guiding others with love, grace, and wisdom.

I humbly ask for your help in seeking guidance in my life,

For there are decisions and paths before me that seem uncertain.

Grant me the grace to trust in God's wisdom and seek His guidance,

That I may walk the path He has prepared for me.

St. Anne, you embraced prayer and reflection,

Finding solace and wisdom in God's presence.

Please pray for me, that I may cultivate a vibrant prayer life,

And seek God's guidance through deep communion with Him.

Help me to discern God's will and align my choices with His plan,

Guiding me to make decisions that honor Him.

May I have the courage to follow His guidance,

Even when the path seems unclear or challenging.

St. Anne, mother and guide of Mary,

Intercede for me before the throne of God.

Obtain for me the grace to seek and follow God's guidance,

That I may navigate life's choices with wisdom and love.

In your loving care, guide me closer to God,

That I may hear His voice and understand His will.

St. Anne, pray for me and all who seek guidance,

That we may trust in God's wisdom and walk the path He has set before us.

Amen.

May this prayer to St. Anne for guidance bring you comfort and clarity as you seek direction in your life. Place your hopes and intentions before her, and ask for her intercession to help you discern God's will and follow His guidance. May her powerful prayers and example of faith and wisdom guide you on the path of righteousness and lead you to make choices that align with God's plan for your life.

Day 8 - The Grace of St. Anne

Reflections on St. Anne's Grace

S t. Anne's grace is a remarkable quality that shines through her life, offering profound reflections for believers. Her grace, rooted in humility and love, serves as an inspiring example for us to contemplate. Here are some reflections on St. Anne's grace:

1. Humble Acceptance: St. Anne's grace was rooted in humble acceptance of God's will. She embraced her role as the mother of Mary and the grandmother of Jesus with humility and gratitude. St. Anne's example challenges us to cultivate a similar attitude of humble acceptance, recognizing that all we have and all we are is a gift from God. By embracing humility, we can receive God's grace and allow it to transform our lives.

2. Unconditional Love: St. Anne's grace was reflected in her unconditional love for her family and all those she encountered. Her love was a source of comfort, strength, and guidance. St. Anne's example encourages us to extend grace and love to others, even in challenging circumstances. By

offering grace-filled love, we can create an atmosphere of compassion, healing, and forgiveness in our relationships.

3. Patience and Resilience: St. Anne's grace was demonstrated through her patience and resilience in the face of trials and difficulties. She endured years of waiting for a child and faced societal pressures with grace. St. Anne's example reminds us that grace enables us to persevere and find strength in the midst of challenges. By embracing grace, we can develop patience and resilience, knowing that God's grace is sufficient to sustain us.

4. Forgiveness and Reconciliation: St. Anne's grace extended to forgiveness and reconciliation. Her grace-filled heart embraced forgiveness, allowing her to restore relationships and foster unity. St. Anne's example challenges us to cultivate a spirit of forgiveness and reconciliation in our own lives. By extending grace through forgiveness, we can experience healing and promote harmony in our relationships and communities.

5. Reflecting God's Grace: St. Anne's grace reflected the grace of God to others. Her life exemplified the transformative power of God's grace, drawing others closer to Him. St. Anne's example calls us to be vessels of God's grace in the world, radiating His love, mercy, and compassion to others. By reflecting God's grace, we can be instruments of His transformative work in the lives of those around us.

Reflecting on St. Anne's grace inspires us to cultivate a similar grace in our own lives. By embracing humble acceptance, offering unconditional love, practicing patience and resilience, extending forgiveness and reconciliation, and reflecting God's grace to others, we can become conduits of God's transformative grace in the world. St. Anne's grace reminds us that through God's grace, we can experience healing, growth, and the abundant life He desires for us.

Prayers for the Eighth Day

Dear St. Anne,

You who embodied grace in its fullest expression,

I come before you seeking your intercession.

You embraced God's will with humility and love,

Radiating grace through your words and actions.

I humbly ask for your help in receiving God's grace,

For there are times when I feel unworthy or lacking.

Grant me the grace to embrace your example of grace,

To open my heart to receive God's abundant grace.

St. Anne, you knew the transformative power of grace,

And your life reflected God's love and mercy.

Please pray for me, that I may open myself to God's grace,

That I may be filled with His love, forgiveness, and healing.

Help me to extend grace to others,

Even when it is difficult or challenging.

May I reflect God's grace in my words and actions,

Creating an atmosphere of love, forgiveness, and reconciliation.

St. Anne, grandmother of Jesus and mother of Mary,

Intercede for me before the throne of God.

Obtain for me the grace to receive God's abundant grace,

To embrace His will and to radiate His love to others.

In your loving care, guide me closer to God,

That I may experience the transformative power of His grace.

St. Anne, pray for me and all who seek God's grace,

That we may be filled with His love, mercy, and compassion.

Amen.

May this prayer to St. Anne for grace uplift and inspire you as you seek to receive God's abundant grace in your life. Place your hopes and intentions before her, and ask for her intercession to help you open your heart to God's grace. May her powerful prayers and example of grace guide you to experience the transformative power of God's love, forgiveness, and healing.

Day 9 - The Intercession of St. Anne

Reflections on St. Anne's Intercession

St. Anne's intercession is a testament to her role as a powerful advocate and mediator before God. Her intercession, rooted in her closeness to God and her love for humanity, offers profound reflections for believers. Here are some reflections on St. Anne's intercession:

1. Motherly Love: St. Anne's intercession reflects her motherly love for al those who seek her help. Just as she cared for her own family with devotion she extends her love and care to all who approach her in prayer. St. Anne': intercession reminds us that she is a compassionate mother figure in th spiritual realm, always ready to lend her ear and offer support.

2. Spiritual Guidance: St. Anne's intercession provides spiritual guidanc and direction to those who seek her help. As the grandmother of Jesus an the mother of Mary, she has a unique closeness to the Holy Family. S

Anne's intercession offers insights and wisdom in navigating life's challenges, pointing us toward the path of righteousness and holiness.

3. Advocacy for Intentions: St. Anne's intercession serves as a powerful advocate for our intentions before God. Just as she interceded for her own needs and desires, she continues to intercede on behalf of those who turn to her for help. St. Anne's intercession reminds us that she stands before God, presenting our prayers and petitions, and asking for His favor and blessings.

4. Miracles and Healing: St. Anne's intercession is associated with numerous accounts of miracles and healings throughout history. Many have experienced her intercession leading to physical, emotional, and spiritual healings. St. Anne's intercession encourages us to approach her with faith and trust, knowing that she can intercede for miraculous interventions in our lives.

5. Deepening Relationship with God: St. Anne's intercession ultimately aims to draw us closer to God. Through her intercession, she desires to lead us into a deeper relationship with God, helping us grow in faith, love, and holiness. St. Anne's intercession reminds us that she is a bridge between us and God, guiding us to a closer union with the Divine.

Reflecting on St. Anne's intercession invites us to approach her with confidence, knowing that she is a loving and compassionate advocate before God. Her intercession reminds us of the power of prayer and the beauty of seeking the intercession of the saints. St. Anne's intercession encourages us to turn to her with our needs, intentions, and desires, trusting in her maternal love and her ability to bring our prayers before God's throne.

Prayers for the Ninth Day

Dear St. Anne,

You who have the privilege of interceding before God,

I come before you seeking your powerful intercession.

You are a loving advocate and a compassionate mother,

Ready to listen to our prayers and present them to God.

I humbly ask for your intercession in my needs and intentions,

Knowing that you have a special closeness to the Holy Family.

Please pray for me and bring my petitions before the throne of God,

That His grace and favor may be bestowed upon me.

St. Anne, you know the challenges and joys of life,

And you understand the desires and struggles of our hearts.

Please intercede for me, that I may find strength, guidance, and healing,

And that I may experience God's loving presence in my life.

In your motherly care, surround me with your love and protection,

And present my prayers to your beloved daughter, Mary,

That she may join her intercession with yours.

May my intentions be heard and answered according to God's will.

St. Anne, mother and advocate, I place my trust in your intercession,

Confident that you will present my prayers to God with love and care.

Thank you for your motherly presence in my life,

And for your powerful intercession on my behalf.

Amen.

May this prayer to St. Anne for intercession strengthen your faith and bring you closer to the grace of God. Place your intentions and needs before her, knowing that she intercedes for you with love and compassion. May her powerful prayers and her closeness to the Holy Family bring forth blessings and favor from our Heavenly Father.

Conclusion

In conclusion, St. Anne holds a significant place in Christian tradition as the grandmother of Jesus and the mother of Mary. Her life is an inspiration for believers, and her intercession is sought for various intentions. Throughout this book, we have explored different aspects of St. Anne's life and her role in our faith. From her virtues of faith, patience, hope, and love to her guidance, grace, and intercession, St. Anne offers us a powerful example of a life devoted to God.

The novena to St. Anne provides us with a structured way to seek her intercession and grow closer to God. Through prayer, reflection, and the nine-day prayer structure, we can deepen our relationship with St. Anne and invite her guidance and blessings into our lives.

As we journey through the novena and reflect on St. Anne's life, we are reminded of the importance of faith, trust, and perseverance in our own spiritual journeys. St. Anne's unwavering devotion to God and her family teaches us to embrace humility, to trust in God's plan, and to seek His guidance in all aspects of our lives. Her intercession offers us hope, strength, and healing as we present our intentions and needs before her.

May the insights and prayers shared in this book serve as a source of inspiration and encouragement as we deepen our devotion to St. Anne. Let us continue to seek her intercession, trust in her guidance, and emulate her virtues in our daily lives. May we be inspired by her example to live lives of faith, love, and grace, drawing ever closer to God and His abundant blessings.

May St. Anne, our loving grandmother in faith, continue to intercede for us, guide us, and lead us to a deeper relationship with God. May her presence in our lives bring us peace, joy, and the knowledge that we are loved and cared for by both her and our Heavenly Father.

May this book, "Novena to St. Anne," be a source of spiritual nourishment and inspiration as we embark on this journey of faith. May it deepen our understanding of St. Anne's life, her virtues, and her intercession, and may it strengthen our connection to her as we seek her help and guidance.

May God's grace and blessings be upon us as we embrace the teachings and intercession of St. Anne, and may our faith be enriched through this novena.

Amen.

Gratitude and Encouragement

As we come to the end of this book on the Novena to St. Anne, let us take a moment to express gratitude and offer words of encouragement.

Firstly, we extend our heartfelt gratitude to St. Anne for her loving presence in our lives and for her intercession on our behalf. We thank her for being a guiding light, a source of strength, and a model of faith and virtue. We are grateful for her unwavering love and care, and we humbly acknowledge the blessings we have received through her intercession.

We also express our gratitude to God for the gift of St. Anne and for the grace and mercy He bestows upon us through her intercession. We recognize that it is by His divine providence that we have come to know and seek the guidance of St. Anne. We thank God for His constant love and faithfulness, and for granting us the opportunity to deepen our faith through this novena.

Furthermore, we extend our gratitude to all those who have joined us on this spiritual journey. Your presence and participation have been instrumental in creating a community of faith and prayer. We are grateful for your support, encouragement, and shared devotion to St. Anne. Together, we have formed a collective voice of prayer, seeking her intercession and growing in our relationship with God.

As we conclude this book, let us be encouraged to continue our devotion to St. Anne beyond these pages. Let us remain steadfast in our faith, trusting in God's guidance and relying on St. Anne's intercession. May the lesson learned, prayers offered, and reflections shared throughout this book inspire us to live lives of deeper faith, love, and grace.

May St. Anne's loving presence continue to guide us, and may our devotion to her deepen with each passing day. Let us remember that we are never alone in our journey of faith, for we have the intercession of St. Anne and the abiding love of our Heavenly Father.

May God bless you abundantly and may St. Anne's intercession bring you comfort, strength, and the fulfillment of your deepest intentions.

With gratitude and encouragement, we conclude this book on the Novena to St. Anne.

Amen.

Continuing Devotion to St. Anne

As we conclude this book on the Novena to St. Anne, let us reflect on the importance of continuing our devotion to her beyond these pages. St. Anne, our beloved grandmother in faith, is always ready to intercede for us and guide us in our spiritual journey. Here are some key points to consider as we continue our devotion to St. Anne:

1. Consistent Prayer: Make it a habit to include St. Anne in your daily prayers. Set aside time to specifically ask for her intercession, express gratitude for her guidance, and seek her maternal care. Whether through the recitation of traditional prayers or personal conversations, let your prayers to St. Anne be a consistent and heartfelt expression of your devotion.

2. Cultivate Virtues: Emulate the virtues that St. Anne exemplified in her life. Foster qualities such as faith, patience, love, and humility. Strive to reflect her grace and selflessness in your interactions with others. By embodying these virtues, you honor St. Anne's legacy and invite her intercession in your life.

3. Seek Guidance: Turn to St. Anne for guidance in your daily decisions and challenges. Trust in her wisdom and experience as a mother and a faithful disciple. Pray for her guidance in navigating difficult situations, discerning God's will, and making choices that align with your faith. Allow her to be a source of counsel and comfort as you seek to live a life pleasing to God.

4. Share Your Devotion: Share your love for St. Anne with others. Spread awareness of her intercession and the graces she bestows. Encourage others to join in the devotion and share their own experiences of her powerful intercession. By sharing your devotion, you contribute to building a community of believers who find solace and inspiration through St. Anne's intercession.

5. Visit Shrines and Pilgrimage Sites: Consider visiting shrines or pilgrimage sites dedicated to St. Anne. These sacred places offer an opportunity for deeper connection and prayer. Engage in pilgrimage to honor her and strengthen your devotion. If physical travel is not possible, participate in virtual pilgrimages or connect with online communities centered around St. Anne.

Remember that devotion to St. Anne is a lifelong journey. Nurture your relationship with her, allowing her to guide you closer to God and inspire you in your faith. With St. Anne's intercession, we find comfort, strength, and a deeper understanding of God's love.

May our devotion to St. Anne continue to flourish, drawing us closer to God and enriching our lives with her maternal care and guidance. May we always seek her intercession, trust in her loving presence, and honor her as a beloved saint and a powerful advocate.

Amen.

Litany to St Anne

Lord, have mercy on us.

Christ, have mercy on us.

Lord, have mercy on us.

Christ, hear us.

Christ, graciously hear us.

God the Father of Heaven, have mercy on us.

God the Son, Redeemer of the world, have mercy on us.

God the Holy Spirit, have mercy on us.

Holy Trinity, one God, have mercy on us.

Holy Mary, pray for us.

St. Anne, pray for us.

St. Anne, filled with grace from your conception, pray for us.

St. Anne, chosen by God to be the mother of Mary, pray for us.

St. Anne, model of faith and obedience, pray for us.

St. Anne, full of compassion and love, pray for us.

St. Anne, faithful and devoted wife of St. Joachim, pray for us.

St. Anne, joyful mother of the Blessed Virgin Mary, pray for us.

St. Anne, guide and protector of your daughter, Mary, pray for us.

St. Anne, example of purity and virtue, pray for us.

St. Anne, teacher of wisdom and faith, pray for us.

St. Anne, intercessor for all who invoke your name, pray for us.

St. Anne, helper in times of need, pray for us.

St. Anne, patroness of mothers and families, pray for us.

St. Anne, comforter of the sorrowful, pray for us.

St. Anne, refuge of the desperate, pray for us.

St. Anne, source of hope and strength, pray for us.

St. Anne, advocate for the unborn, pray for us.

St. Anne, protector of marriage and family life, pray for us.

St. Anne, patroness of workers and laborers, pray for us.

St. Anne, model of perseverance and trust in God, pray for us.

St. Anne, whose prayers are powerful before the throne of God, pray for us.

St. Anne, who received the honor of being the grandmother of Jesus, pray for us.

St. Anne, our loving grandmother in faith, pray for us.

Lamb of God, who takes away the sins of the world, spare us, O Lord.

Lamb of God, who takes away the sins of the world, graciously hear us, O Lord.

Lamb of God, who takes away the sins of the world, have mercy on us.

Pray for us, St. Anne, that we may be made worthy of the promises of Christ.

Let us pray:

O God, the Father of our Lord Jesus Christ, who chose St. Anne to be the mother of the Blessed Virgin Mary and the grandmother of our Savior, grant us the grace to imitate her virtues and seek her intercession in our needs. May her example of faith, purity, and love inspire us to follow her path of holiness. Through Christ our Lord. Amen.

Note: This litany is a traditional prayer, and you may adapt or personalize it according to your preferences and intentions.

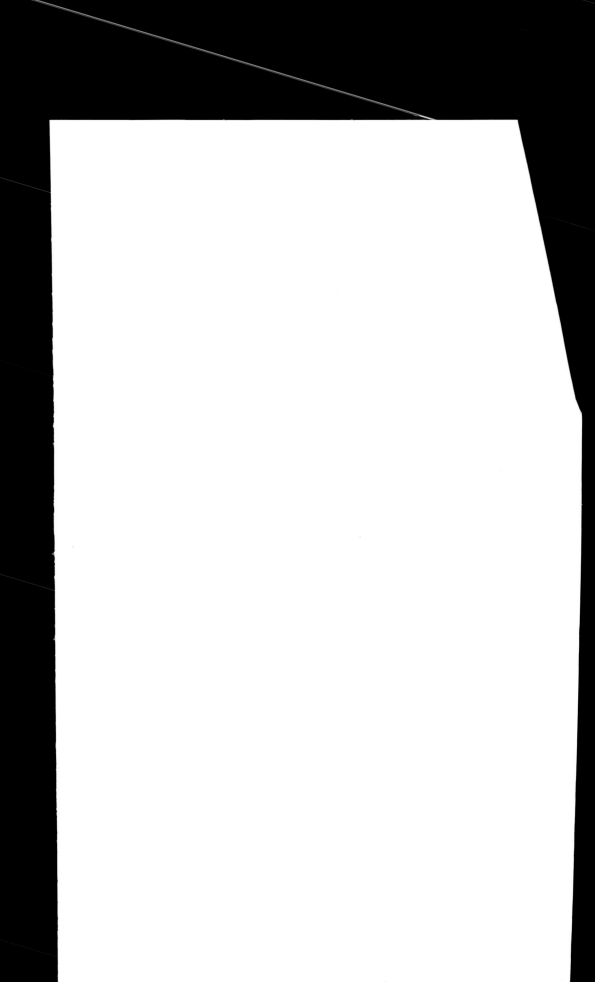

Printed in Great Britain
by Amazon